GATHERING EVIDENCE:
(The Evidence of Things Not Said)

Essays and Diaries collection

Tendai Rinos Mwanaka

Mwanaka Media and Publishing Pvt Ltd,
Chitungwiza, Zimbabwe
*
Creativity, Wisdom, and Beauty

Publisher: *Mmap*
Mwanaka Media and Publishing Pvt Ltd
24 Svosve Road, Zengeza 1
Chitungwiza, Zimbabwe
mwanaka@yahoo.com
mwanaka13@gmail.com
https://www.mmapublishing.org
www.africanbookscollective.com/publishers/mwanaka-media-and-publishing
https://facebook.com/MwanakaMediaAndPublishing/

Distributed in and outside N. America by African Books Collective
orders@africanbookscollective.com
www.africanbookscollective.com

ISBN: 978-1-77933-145-8
EAN: 9781779331458

© Tendai Rinos Mwanaka 2024

All rights reserved.
No part of this book may be reproduced or transmitted in any form or by any means, mechanical or electronic, including photocopying and recording, or be stored in any information storage or retrieval system, without written permission from the publisher

DISCLAIMER
All views expressed in this publication are those of the author and do not necessarily reflect the views of *Mmap*.

Gathering Evidence
Diaries (2013-2014)

Wednesday 1 January 2013

I have never had such a terribly painful and boring Christmas period as the last one I have just had. I spent most of my time dealing with stress, illness (cholesterol) and general angst. Last year was a good year for me but for those last few days. But I am through it all. I am feeling better now
*****

It was raining since 6 in the morning. It's almost midday now. It has stopped raining. The temperatures are a beautiful cloudy. I like it! I like it! I like it!
*****

Yesterday I started the 10 days of fasting. There are 10 days of fasting and prayer directed by our parish priest, father Joseph Matare, in which we will be meeting at the church for the prayers, talks and Mass. I have shied away from participating in these 10 days before, for the last 2 years since they were introduced but this year I am in. I feel I want to develop a closer relationship with myself, with God. I have doubted whether my relationship with God is still good, for years now, so I would like to push it to become closer. I still talk or pray regularly to God but I feel stunted or as if I am in a comfort zone with him. I need to feel him more, better, closer. There is more I want, would like to achieve on. It's about me, too. Sometimes I feel I have lost my way; that I am getting more lost with every day; that I don't feel closer to myself as I used to do. There is mostly too much psychic (not too dark, though…, just that kind that's restless and frustrating) traffic, sometimes I have really bad vibes with myself and it's all these I am trying to deal with. It was all these things I was trying to think about during the Christmas time and I wasn't getting headway.

I felt so lonely as if I had travelled too far and I have forgotten my way back, home (in the sense of a place that makes you grounded and happy). I have also been writing or thinking on this idea that I am now hitting at 40 this year, and that I should be making my way, or on the way to finding my way home. A couple of days or so ago I watched Toni Morrison (American writer) being interviewed about her latest novel, HOME, on F24, by Em Jackson, saying the home could be , *there is no home at all*. It's like negating a negative to find a positive. Morrison felt there was no home, and if there was no home, she was trying, in her novel, to construct such a home for herself. It's like the concept of trying to build something from negating everything until you get to where it all started. I am thinking, I have been thinking I am now on the way to finding my own home. I have thought about this and I have been writing about it, too. I don't want it to be philosophical or ideological or even a literary take of it. I want to really experience it. Sometimes I feel there is a bigger part of me I have frozen over the years and haven't explored that much and in this journey I would like to unfold, unfreeze these parts. I have to really know this part of me and these 10 days of fasting might also afford me an opportunity to figure out what parts of my life I need to unfreeze, to explore. One that easily comes to my mind and might be the most important thing is on relationships. It's no longer about me and a girl relationship. It's pretty much about all facets of relationships. I feel I have been lagging, sometimes quiet terribly. I don't have close relationships with my friends anymore, and I am not making much effort anymore, rather it is them who are trying

harder to stay closer to me. With my family it is improving but it needs more working on. With a partner, it is disappointing. I really need this to start working. I have tried a lot of girls around, this last year without much. It's still there is no relationship worth talking of; they are always flirting out of my life like mayflies. I feel like I am running circles around the beginnings of relationships and then that's that, no growing of these relationships to really enjoy them. I want to do the journeying with a girl, enjoying the ups and downs of it all and get to something. I want to be walking. I need more, but the journey is static.
*****

I want to make the journey. I am going to make the journey. I want to settle down someday soon, and this year, if possible. I want to continue with the journey in different aspects of my life. I want to discover me, to find my home. Now, it's the journey to find my way, to discover what my home is, with whom, I don't know.
*****

In the fasting, I am doing a gradual fasting, or immersion into it. Today I am fasting up to at least mid day. Then I want to push it further tomorrow until I can fast for longer periods. I have always had issues about fasting, some of which I explored indirectly in the essay, THE HUNGER STRIKE in the collection of nonfictions and essays, *Zimbabwe: The Blame Game*, 2013. We are working with the editor and publisher Roselyn Jau to have this book published, and the process is taking more of my time. It's a journey I am going to make this year too, having the book published!
*****

I want us to work things out with Colleen (it's a pseudonym I am going to use). I have to find some way to work things with her. At least try to push or pull for a relationship and see how things will pan out. Despite some couple of things I don't like about her, I think she is a good girl. I can feel the potential in her. Is it a job? It's another of the journeys I will be making this year
*****

13.00 pm
I am so hungry!
*****

I am about to turn in now for the night. It's roughly past 9 at night. I attended Mass and the fasting programme at the church. It was one of the best Mass and prayer I have had in years. I talked and talked to God about the issues I have highlighted in this diary. I felt very close to him. I am about to turn in. what's left are night prayers
*****

Oh! Before I close for the day, today I was sogged down to the bone with rain, a deluge when coming back home from the church. It rained hard from about 5 pm up to now (9pm), it's still raining. I am unfazed by all that. If it rains badly tomorrow again, the same time, it is going to rain me down as I return from church, again. If this is going to be happening to me for the rest of the fasting time, bring it on! I even feel cleansed by all these rains…and very happy.
****

Let me pray!

Thursday 3 January 2013

I am happy with myself, I think quiet happy. When I am happy with myself I write a lot. I have just written a travel article, *My Volmoed Journey*, on my journey to South Africa for the Caine workshop, in March 2012. For the whole of last year I couldn't get it going, but for the last few hours ago I have written and completed it. Friends next door, Catherine and Carol are back from holidaying with their Uncles and Aunts in South Africa. I have talked to them. I missed them. It's nice to see them.
****

Last night I had a fun dream. I had travelled to some place. I don't even remember, why. When I arrived at the place, which I thought, at that first moment of dreaming, as a local place I know, I discovered it was frozen in ice. It was a dam frozen, and another part was a lake, which at first wasn't frozen. I thought of crossing it, I don't know if it was because of fear but I told myself I could take the long way and cross it off at the top end where it ends. I had to be on the other side of it, so I obsessed about it and loitered around the frozen dam. Later the lake was frozen, too. The place resembled Volmoed in South Africa, the environment of it but it felt like it was somewhere else. At one time I am trying to finish off some writing. I am at the workshop where I have to produce a story. I am very confident I am going to produce a really good story. I obsess a lot on top of this ice. I get paid some money for the story. It was in pounds sterling. I am happy. Eventually I tell myself I have to take the path across this lake, even though I have already crossed it several

times in my obsessiveness whilst it was iced. I take the journey and then I wake up
*****

I am continuing with my fasting. The idea is I have to eat little and start eating after 12 pm everyday. Of course I am hungry, but I am okay. I am happy. Does fasting make one happy? I will read the bible, I love reading the book of Romans, and I will pray in the afternoons before eating. Later I will attend prayers and Mass at the church, St. Agnes Catholic Church, Zengeza, Chitungwiza, which is in Zengeza 3

Saturday 5 January 2013

It's raining and raining, damp, very nice. It rained throughout the night. It is about to rain. I miss her. I last saw her last Sunday. I like her a lot. I tell myself I want this. Isn't most of it about telling yourself you need someone, want to be with someone, only that one person.
*****

I am continuing with my fasting and prayers and it's the 5th day. A couple of days ago there was talk of Christianity and the family. The priest, father Matare, talked of love between family members that got me arrested and interested. He said parents should not choose or show favouritism toward children, and that they should treat children equally. Then someone asked how can a parent balance out love, and what if it's the child that is feeling she is being sidelined when in actual fact the parent doesn't think or feel they were doing that. Father Matare said the fact that a kid feels that way should be of cause of concern to the parent. A parent should try to make or work toward making the kid not to feel that way. It should not be about how the parent feels about things but what the kid feels the parent is doing. It's a tough call but very much interesting. He even pointed out the kind of sick, destructive rivalry that will result from all that if it's not sorted out by referring to the story of Joseph in the bible, who was sold out by his brothers to the Egyptians because of this sibling rivalry created through favouritism. It's a difficult thing to practice and contemplate on. God in the bible showed favouritism to Isaac, and to many others. I don't think it's possible to love two different people, equally. Is it possible? Favouritism will show out no matter how much you might not try to show it.

Another very interesting aspect he also touched on is there is as much each family can try to pray for unity, love or togetherness. He said sometimes we just have to accept that it is not working and that our families are meant to be that disfigured or hellholes, and try to live with that. He said we have to accept that crucifix and carry it every day. It's another tough call, but I think I understand that.

*****

Generally I am great with myself, feel very close to myself and my creator.

Friday 11 January 2013

The fasting is over. It ended yesterday. It was hugely successful for me for I am very happy with myself. I feel more connected to myself, connected to God. I feel settled into myself. I know I am going to face this year well. I have dealt with all the fears and toxic doubts I had about myself and others. I believe I love Colleen but I am also ready to let her go if she wants me to go. That's now what I am working on. I want to know if she wants me to go. Then I will go. It's a sad fact of life and I would if it were to be done in another way. I have learned, if you love someone you should be willing to let them go when they want to go.

*****

It's slightly windy, and humid. It rained yesterday last night, so it isn't that hot, but humid. I feel a bit restless. I have talked to her a bit. At least it seems she is now listening to me or trying to hear what I am saying, even though she doesn't always get it right. It's good to know she is trying to understand or just listening and talking to me. All that I want is for us to always be able to talk to each other despite what will become of us now. Talk is always good.

*****

My heart is bursting with love for her; I feel like an unused, disused pit hole, no one wants to pile their shit in it. I want to tell her these words, "I love you, I love you, I love you…", until she understands the hell of it!

Thursday 17 January 2013

This state I am in, this place, this situation I am in possesses me like a monster demon. I have struggled to get free from it without success. It is because I am afraid of the outside environments of this situation, this life. How could I be afraid when I want to go there, to get to that outside? I am single, lonely single. I don't seem to hold a girl down to relationship worth talking about. I am always trying, and be more willing to try more. It's frustrating, defeating to realise she didn't stick a bit longer on me, to me, in me. I am running against myself- a lot of the times, to make it out with these girls. I feel I am corroding my inner true self-worth to hold these down, and even that don't seem enough. I am tired of my condition. Is it a shadow I can't seem to walk away from…yet I want to walk into someone and stay inside that someone.

Tuesdays 22 January 2013

Yesterday something extraordinary (maybe unusual is the right word here) happened in Chitungwiza. I hope it would change people's lives here permanently, profoundly maybe. It was somewhere after mid-afternoon, the sky was with very few fluffy clouds. I was restless, so I was reading a bit trying to hold down that restlessness; sometimes I tried to think or to write something without success and some other times slept, dozed off for most of the day, and then all of a sudden, *boom*…, like a bomb or something like that. It wasn't like an earthquake shake or tremours. I remembered when somewhere Kariba dam had a tremor and we felt it all the way in my rural home in Nyanga, over 500 km from Kariba, so I knew the tremours of the earth's sneezes. It wasn't, it was more like lightening, more like a bomb, and it was surprising to hear that sound in the clear skies, worse to think of it as a bomb sound in Chitungwiza. I woke up from my dozing position, got outside, and checked around the street, everyone was doing the same. There was nothing in the street. It had happened further than our street. People started speculating, some rushed-off to the source.

I returned back to my dozing meditation position and environment, still I had no inspiration for anything. I didn't sleep or meditated longer as the stories started piercing my worlds, unravelling what had happened. Some saying it was a bomb, some saying it was a gas stove, some saying a lot of people had died. Yes, it had happened in Zengeza 2, at number 4 Ndororo Street, just a house off the corner of Ndororo Street and Mukomberanwa drive, on the way to Zengeza 3. Those who witnessed it said there were a strong wind and an explosion that shook this household and others surrounding it, breaking down and cracking houses around this place, 4 men and a small kid died. These four included a business man (taxi operator) who owned the *Barcelona* fleet of taxis, whom it seems, had come to consult a N'anga (tradition faith healer), whom some said had also come from somewhere, a week before. It is said whilst this N'anga was doing his treatment ceremony on this businessman that's when a lightning struck the place. The general accepted version in the gossip torn streets is that a lightning struck this place, and that it is seeded lightening, by this N'anga or someone else, maybe someone the businessman and N'anga wanted to hurt. In our culture or tradition there is a belief that some N'angas can manufacture (or engineer) a lightning strike, even in clear skies like yesterday's skies and can use this to struck off enemies, and so this is the version that was propagating rapidly. Even in the news at 8, the national broadcaster, *Zimbabwe Television* reported the incident much the same way, speculatively.

The speculation is now it's either this businessman wanted to hurt someone, or he wanted to disposes himself of some Tokoloshis (half human, half monster beings) used to help accrue wealth with, that had helped him accumulate the wealth he had (the taxi fleet), and that the N'anga wasn't strong enough and was overpowered by these Tokoloshis. It's a massive gossip and speculating realm now opened up in Chitungwiza, and the entire country. The people I stay with (who lodges some rooms at our place), when it happened they were travelling back to the city from their rural homes after an extended end of year holiday there, but when they arrived home they already knew a lot about it, even more than I knew who was in the area when it happened. They say some relative, in Rusape town, 200kms from here had called them, telling them of this spectacle. It is how gossip flies off the shelves in Zimbabwe, like scarce commodities.

I know this Sunday, in the churches around Chitungwiza and Zimbabwe; the bible thumpers are going to have a great go at this story. Either way you look at it, it shows massive promise to make it into the churches; comparing God's power over us mortals will be the point of entry of every sermon. I don't want to be preachy but I feel, I would like to think it would put a lot of things into perspective. Those who are still looking for wealth through these shoddy means are going to think twice before consulting a N'anga again. Those who think they are very powerful spiritually, like the motley lot of these N'angas and the prophetic faith healers that are ubiquitous all over the country are going to be very careful. Or they are going to be more daring. There is a challenge in this episode. Chitungwiza is now a battleground between different opposing spiritual worlds. There are a lot of bible thumpers and prophetic man of God doing crazy miracles, even the inappropriately popular prophet Makandiwa has located his church from Harare to Chitungwiza, and is on the forefront of this miracle making madness.

A few months ago he was said to have made bald headed people have their hair back in their heads. Another prophet, Eubert Angels was said to be putting money into his congregant's pockets, miraculously. And who wouldn't want to go a church where instead of the church man taking your hard earned toil, rather you are given

what you never earned. It's like manna from heaven. I think most of the miracles are crazy miracles, stupid hoodwinking jobs to attract more attention and more rent from the desperate people of Chitungwiza. My exuberant priest, father Lovemore Gutu, in last Sunday's homily said if someone can be able to put money into your pocket or account or cell phone account, he can also be able to take money from you, thus he was attacking Eubert Angels. These supposed prophets are super rich and still counting. It might boil down to Chitungwiza is the poorest of all Zimbabwean cities. It is a ghetto hell hole of very poor people, but all the same, ambitious. This is like a cooking pot for creating the drive or ambition to succeed and vault one's self off this city. Thus Chitungwiza is a hotbed of talents in different fields in the country. You can say without being wrong that Chitungwiza gave Zimbabwe half of talents in the following among other fields; Music, all art fields, all sports, media talents, technical talents. If you raise from this dunk city and become successful it is a classic case of from rugs to riches, and since there are not many opportunities in the city itself, people are now resorting to getting wealth through shoddy means, exemplified by the 4 Ndororo street episode, the Makandiwas et el. It's a battleground for evil and good- it seems a lot now think it's the only way to get head over their poverty, through evil. I am sorry I was a bit preachy, but it is an interesting, very interesting place to live in, as well. I will unravel this story as it grips us here.
****

It's humid hot, a summer day and everything is going on the usual way here. I am fine, still hung up with personal stuff. There is someone who is attracting my attention, whom I knew a couple of years ago, and I had given up on her, the Miss K in IT'S NOT ABOUT ME dairies. I am sure I DON'T want this in my life again. It was one of those things that possessed me yesterday and also I had seen Colleen at the church on Sunday. It was the quietest feeling I have had over a girl that I had with her on Sunday. She came to greet me and I was polite with her. But yesterday I thought of her (stubbornly, my mind doesn't seem to stop). I am conflicted. It's a complex situation. I still have feelings for her, and its hurting me bad. I think she is hurting, as well. But I don't know, whatever!

*****

Yesterday on the news there was a tentative announcement from Kgalema Motlanthe (South African president) who is the mediator in the talks between the MDC and ZANU-PF that there has been common ground between the two parties on the constitution making endeavour. That very soon it would be presented to the parliament and the people for voting and a referendum. It's interesting to hear this. I am not sure what common ground has been found, since the two parties had divergent views on a lot of issues they couldn't agree on in the draft. Has ZANU-PF bite the humble pie and allowed for the power diluting draft they were so set against all through the whole of last year, or has the MDC sold out on the people's wishes and expectations for power mongering reasons. I need to know what the compromises are. Zimbabwe feels, everyday, like a lost cause. I don't know, I have not much faith we will ever reach Nirvana land with these political players we have. We have already given up on a lot of things that we fought for the last 10 years or so and we can only lose so much more with this constitution until a time when it's not worth it. We seem to be heading towards that point.

Wednesday 23 January 2013

The plot thickens and the stories are abounding and deepening. I am no longer happy in writing this diary anymore, because it has become personal. I know the owners of 4 Ndororo Street. I have been friends; we are distant relatives with them. I have known the daughter of this place for years, somewhere in the late 1990s, she rented (with her cousin brother's family) some rooms next door, and that's when we got to know each other. With my sisters they are still very close. We call her sister Via (for Violet) and it was disturbing to hear it had happened at their place. At first, just the term 4 Ndororo street had tagged something in my mind, but I couldn't figure out what it was, until my sister, Judith, came through my place last night and reminded me it was sister Via's family home, and then everything became clear to me. I knew why, all along, something was wrong and I had wrongfully assigned it to relationships. It was this that was obsessing me. I get to feel like that when something bad is going to happen. A street friend, Prosper Mlambo came through an hour after it had happened. He wanted to pick me up so as to accompany him to the place to see what was really happening and I had said, no. I told him it might be the place of someone I know or I might see someone I know maimed or dead and I didn't want that. Delayed knowledge of a disaster somehow seem to prepare you to better face it, as long as you generally know something has happened and you don't know who has been affected, yet. It is the time to get to terms with any eventuality, such that when you know that there is someone you know who has been a victim of it, then you have already prepared to face it. I knew then, something was wrong, and that's why I refused to go. Only to now realise last night that I knew all along. It is the place of someone I know. None of the dead though or the maimed are part of this family. What follows is hurtful for me to write. I need time to process this discovery. I still feel restless, like I am living outside my skin.

Thursday 24 January 2013

I am assaulted by theories, plots, gossips… Chitungwiza is abounding with it, sizzling with talk of it. People are talking madly around this issue. I think we have moved from the initial shock part and people are trying to figure out what really happened at number 4 Ndororo Street. I will keep using this title of 4 Ndororo Street to remove myself from personal connections of it, and it is now a mythical, enigmatic name, even though it's just a place I have known. Here is another story. Sometime beginning of this month, on the 6th January, their long time tenant for 12 years disappeared without giving notice of leave, or a forwarding address, so the rooms became vacant. This departing lodger owed my relatives over $1 000 in United States terms, and that's a fortune in Zimbabwe, so they decided to disappear. These relatives decided to replace the disappeared tenant with others. They were two well-groomed guys, suited to the hilt, who came looking for a place for their brother. The owners of 4 Ndororo Street asked them where that brother was, and they said he was bogged down with other stuff, and was coming from another town, far away and that's why they took the duty of helping him secure lodgings. Not knowing they were creating problems for themselves, these relatives of mine took these people's money and gave them the place to stay. On 10th January the tenant came with his family. Nobody had told my relatives this tenant was a N'anga, only to discover it as he had settled in, as people started coming from all over the country looking for this N'anga, being helped with their problems. The father of my relatives was staying in the rural areas and when he heard of this he came to Chitungwiza from Nyanga where he stays to give notice of evacuation by month end to this new tenant. The day he left for home is the day the property, 4 Ndororo street went up in flames, taking with it 5 lives, including an innocent 1 month old tot, a kid of one of the lodgers, an innocent tenant. Here are the ghoulish details.

The woman, the businessman's wife and the other tenants said there was this huge white wind that shook up things and the N'anga was stirring his medicine clay pot. In that wind, they said they saw a black thing with white lips, the purported Tokoloshi the businessman wanted to part with in this ceremony. The woman run out as the place was struck by a bolt, some say of lightening, and some say even the N'anga was hit off when he tried to run out. The 5 were cut into pieces. The businessman's scalp was found hung on top of the roofs; pieces of flesh were sprayed all over the property. When the fire brigade came they had to concentrate on picking up of the pieces, jumping over licking blood, splattered all over the place.

Those who survived included the wife of the N'anga, the businessman's wife and the mother of the kid and they denied there was a Tokoloshi dumping ceremony, even the relatives of the N'anga are saying he is not a N'anga as such but a faith healer of the apostolic sect known as Johann Nguwo Tsvuku (Johann of red cloth). Yet this sect is known of practicing both traditional and Christian rituals, and they believe in an eye for an eye. This sect came out of the original, larger apostolic sect, Johann weChishanu (Johann of Friday). Some people were saying the Tokoloshi is the one that killed all these people and it drank their blood as revenge for this dumping ceremony. In our culture they are thought, said to do so, especially for killing their benefactors. No one knows for sure whether the Tokoloshi left.

The biggest part of my mind screams, NO, to all these explanations. Yes there might be this ceremony, yes there was the N'anga, yes a lot of it is correct traditionally, but I can't seem to bite all these ideas. There has to be a bomb involved, somehow. The police and bomb experts are with me on this. They believe there was an incendiary bomb which would explain the noise destructions and the burns. The question is who planted it, and why set it to explode the same time this N'anga was doing his ceremony. Was this bomb also targeted at this businessman or the N'anga, or even owners of this place? But for whatever reason. There are a lot of questions that need answering
*****

I am told they finally took the corpses (I mean the pieces, for I am not sure if they identified every piece and assigned each piece to its actual owner, since they were mixed up after the blast. What did the relatives of these people salvaged and buried? Did they bury their relatives, or a bit of each of the other 4 dead) to the mortuary, a day after it had happened. A huge contingency of security establishment (police, riot police, army, CIO) guarded the place and are still guarding the place as it swells with people coming from all over the country, coming to see number 4 Ndororo Street. It's a national security issue I suppose, especially with the issue of the bomb being the real deal, thus I suppose that's why the national security agents are also there. I haven't been there, and I still don't want to visit it.

It's now a mythical place for me. It is also a blood spot. I don't like seeing human blood, especially dead people's blood. The blood possesses me and I don't seem to know how to communicate with it. I remember some years ago (1999) when we were involved in an accident on our way to Botswana, on a trade endeavour there. We grinded down a small car under the bus we were travelling in, and the bus crashed the driver of this car into mince meat. I had to watch as the police collected this mincemeat into plastic bag, whilst trying to prise the car from under the bus, and blood oozing out. It took me many years to deal with that. The picture is still there but now it doesn't possess me, obsessing me as it used to do. I didn't want to create another one by visiting this place of bloodbath at 4 Ndororo Street. Someday I will come close to it, but not now. I will stubbornly refuse its enticements. I will write this from some distance
*****

Like I said, Chitungwiza is abuzz with conspiracies, gossips, plots…, just now I heard a huge snake was found in a taxi at the local bus stop as people abandoned it on the road, fleeing away from this snake. Is this snake another Tokoloshi? The taxi operators, like the above businessman, are known to have Tokoloshis in the form of snakes. Is this another Tokoloshi or it's just a ruse, or maybe just a lost snake that found its way accidentally into this vehicle.
*****

Some NGOs, including the local council people were cleaning and clearing up the place, 4 Ndororo Street yesterday, removing the rubble, pitching tents, feeding people who were affected. I hope someone would help them reconstruct their homes and lives. The most disturbing effects of this is that the nearby children, from properties around this place, feel haunted, needed help to deal with the effects of this happening. The children are said to be afraid of getting outside their houses and play. This is one of the far reaching effects of such a thing. It might be what I am avoiding as well by refusing to visit this place. It will colonise me like it has done to these kids. It will take years and years before they do away with it. I hope there is some psychologist who will help these kids or the most affected to deal with this.

Friday 25 January 2013

I had a heart wrenching dream last night. I was dreaming we were going to an activity at the church youth group level. At one time I was saying I don't have money and won't be going but still I couldn't stop going. I kept going. She followed me. I am talking of Colleen, somehow she wasn't sure where I stood with her, so she kept coming, even though she didn't want to- and then I entered the event area, an enclosure, off a water point. It wasn't an intimidating water point, for there were lots of sands, and shallow waters. I kept getting in and I was almost there when I decided to check where she was. She was saying goodbye to a friend. She couldn't proceed in, she didn't have the license to keep following me in. and then she started retracing her footsteps back. She was so dejected, so lonely, so defeated, so desolate... My heart churned for her, clanged like a lonesome bell. I couldn't take it anymore so I started running out of this place for her. I felt I had to be with her and then I woke up. I felt gutted, so gutted with emotions and feelings. It took me some time for me to deal with this dream and the feelings it brought to me. I didn't even know if the dream had continued whether I was going to catch up with her and soften the pain, and tell her how much I loved her. Was she going to understand me this time?
****

After digesting it for some time I realise I have to be open for her. I have to be patient with her. I have to wait for her, just a bit. And if she reaches out, I have to embrace her. I had been thinking of moving on to another girl but I think I need to wait a bit. It's my heart that is telling me to do so, or maybe I am doing that thing again,

of trying to construct that which my psyche knows is not there so that I could deal well with the fact or the place that it should be.
*****

I think I had a terrible day today. There is this too self-important person I tried to get into contact with over payments, outstanding since last November, of my novel I sold to him (Keys in the River), who is also a church mate and I have known him for years and years. He has always looked down on me, self-importantly. I could have worked into a rivalry of some sort with him but I always shied away from it. There is a time, years ago, when we liked the same girl and we jostled against each other in trying to win her. The girl liked me and I got her and he never liked it. But since we have been around each other for years we grew to respect each other, I don't know any other term to use here. He bought my novel, he wanted to read me. Today I had to wait for him for over 2 hrs in Harare city centre, and he still couldn't call to let me know what was holding him up. My phone had no airtime, I was broke… I only had bus fare back to Chitungwiza so I went to my former workplace, Amtec Motors in 4th street to borrow airtime from my former boss, only to call him and he now wanted me to take a taxi to his home, in the outskirts Avenue area of Harare city centre. I didn't have the money and the energy to keep chasing him through Harare. I think it was just a game with him, like I was his playing with monkey, laughing at me. I told him, brutally, to keep the money. I am no longer interested in the money, for I have wasted a lot in trying to get it. If I take the money he will be paying me for the expenses of trying to get it and my wasted time, not for the work, the tears, and the sweat I poured in creating the book. It seems he thinks he is so important and everyone has to run around for him, and everyone else's jobs, careers and homes, or even lives are not as important as his. I have had enough of his buffoonery, and self-important attitude with me, so I told him to keep it.

Tuesday 12 February 2013

It's a long leap into the month of February without writing anything. I am stunted. I am bored, frustrated, just submerged. I need a breakthrough. Colleen is making my life a hell hole. I need a prayer and a wingman to get through to her. I am at the end of my tether.

Wednesday 20 February 2013

It has been an emotional roller coaster for me for the last 3 months, trying to deal with my feelings for her. I am done with her but there is still a lot of soul searching, the mind, heart, soul. We always try to figure out where it went wrong. There is realisation in me that I have lost out on her. Funnily, not to anyone this time around, for she says she is still single. She doesn't want to be with me, period. It has to do with me, its fine. I am cool with all this. I know I can get rejected, and I will take it well. There is cutting, a necessary tearing in me, but I will connect the pieces, eventually. I will be fine.

***

I haven't been focusing well on my work for some time. I think for 2 weeks or so. Before that I completed a long short story of plus 6 000 words, WHEN HE WAS STILL CLOSER HOME, inside a week. It's a memoir story of my earliest life until when I was about 7. I can't say I completed it, for I want to continue writing it in another time, but I think I have enough for it to stand as a story of its own now. I am writing again, mostly poetry around the collection, A PORTRAIT OF. Last year I didn't write more than 5 poems for the entire year, didn't do much diarising for it was my off-year. I didn't place much poetry into journals and lit places too. I have been doing that for 4 days now, with overwhelming responses and acceptances, so I am a bit excited.

****

My heart says yes, it is a yes. When it says saying no… it should be a no. I am trying to defy it, a bit this time. It doesn't give me much leeway. Maybe it's my mind that does that to me, I don't know how to separate the two, sometimes.

*****

Its midday and it is so hot. If there was no clarity in my thoughts, today should have been a miserable day for me. I have just been working on some poems; I did 3 poems today, so altogether I have tallied over 16 poems for the past week or so. It means it's becoming a sizable or significant work. Another collection I have been working on is this diary collection. I have to decide on the titled between COLLECTING (GATHERING) EVIDENCE. But I have been accumulating the diaries, over 20 now. Another collection is that of short stories around the idea I have been toying around on for some time, even in the poems, dairies etc…, it's about finding one's path to home, so this story collection is entitled FINDING A WAY HOME (I think I have about 15 000 words altogether now). A collection of essays on language, art, thought and existence aptly entitled, LANGUAGE, ART, THOUGHT AND EXISTENCE is another collection I am working on. It's more like a writer's journey around these issues, not necessarily an academic take of it; a journey through life, a journey into places, into worlds, into ideas. These are the 4 works I have settled into working on this year. My intention is to have them completed by end of year, a tall order. It means when things get hire-wire in relationship terms, I can always nudge myself back to reality by focusing on any one of these. There are other works I am working on, already completed but just needing a nudge here and there, a diary collection, IT'S NOT ABOUT ME (2010-2011 dairies) that I am typing slowly, and RAGE OF DEVILS, a play that needs a lot of working on. I will try to put in some work onto these too. I am also into a lot of photography but it's still for the love of it.

Monday 25 Feb 2013

I had a date with Kudzai today. I know it's sudden to start this diary like this because she feels suddenly there, in this group of diaries, in my life. No, she is not. I have known her for 6 plus years. We talked about getting together 3 months ago, and I couldn't get it going then, I was embroiled in another girl Colleen. I didn't want to start something, to write about her, yet. But today I would write a note about her. I enjoyed her company, she is a good conversationist unlike Colleen. I have said I don't want to jump the gun again, so I will leave it at this. I need to work through stuff, through it all, for me to come to clarity, to start saying too much

Thursday 28 Feb 2013

It's the last day of the month. I like February, without the valentine nonsense. It is always a short month, especially after the difficult long January. January disease. Being broke after spending too much in December holidays. . February is a welcome thing. Instantly you find yourself in March. And March is when you want to know what you are capable of achieving for the year. I have a lot of things I want to achieve on and I am on the go already, so I have to keep on the ball, for the rest of the year to see them through. Last week, on Thursday I started editing my book, *Zimbabwe The Blame Game*, on my own. If I don't do that I won't have it published this year. The publisher had assigned me the task to find someone who could read and edit it for me. I have approached a couple of people Kevin Halligan and Nicky Elam and both are busy and have been giving me excuses as I check on the progress. So I realized the best I could do is to have a stab on it on my own. They are busy. I have accumulated some editing skills from my last novel, *Keys in the River*, editorial processes with my editors, Zach and Jennie Oliver and publisher Daniel Janik, so I am utilizing these skills here. I think I can do it. I am doing it.

Friday 1 March 2013

I feel awesome. Kudzai visited me last night- about 7 in the evening. We messed around some fun, no we did not, what young people call it now, smash. We just had fun, she is a warm lover. I am going to enjoy this, what did Jada Pinkett call it, entanglement…

Last night I had a huge dream. I don't know what it means. I was at my Auntie's place, my mother's older sister, Maiguru Mapatirisha, mother of my cousin Patricia, in Nyanga. We stay close, less than 500mtrs from each other, there are a couple of homes between us. I didn't remember why I had gone there. I saw my Auntie, she was in her kitchen hut, so I got outside, I think I was leaving and then I realized my Uncle, my Auntie's Husband was around at the far end where he did his sculptures. He was talking to two white men who had white hair. I didn't know them. So I greeted them and all of a sudden there was a commotion. I ran off into one of the houses, room…it felt like as if the runs we would have during liberation war time when we were little. My uncle fought in the liberation war. There were other people inside these rooms who had seek shelter. These other people, two of them opened the window overlooking the east, jumped outside and sneaked down toward Nyajezi River. At one time I thought I should do so, could do that but I stayed put. Then I realized I was alone in the room and the outside was now quiet. Eventually I must have left the room. I looked around me, outside the place was now surrounded by very tall beautiful trees, arranged artistically. I didn't know the name of these trees. But I saw a baobab, and another thorny tree (black wattle). They were creating wonderful sights for the eyes, and I was walking around them enjoying them, amazed. I even told uncle that the place was so beautiful, that he could even turn the place into a park. He accepted that…then eventually I must have left the place. I didn't know what this dream meant.

Some months later, in September, my Uncle died

Someone once told me that if you dream a dream with white people in it, it means there were witches involved. Witches I am told take a white man's face if they are trying to bewitch a person they know so that they could never be recognized. I must have been visited last night or were they bewitching my uncle?

I am not really scared of witches anymore. Yes when we were little the thought of witches could literally freeze us in fear. I don't think they are effective now. I don't believe in this nonsense. So, I don't feel bothered by this dream. I am in a wonderful world and Kudzai makes me feel so good. I have to hold a girl like that.

Today its sticky hot, I wish it could rain…it hasn't rained in a long while. Everything is crying for a little rain. Even me too

Friday March 8, 2013

It's a boring day, but I am good. I have received an offer from Langaa for the book of essays, The Blame Game. I signed off 2 days ago, and now its official. It is coming out this year in Cameroon. We have entered typesetting print setting stage. I have supplied the bio and back cover blurb and front page photo suggestion, so it's on the go any day. There is not much I will get from the whole book deal, the publisher seemed to have squeezed me of every right, but I am willing to give in to create publishing track record, and add up to my earnings in these deals, and learn the skills. I am still early in my career, we don't have a lot of choices, so I am willing to take this

Saturday 16 March 2013

I have just exercised my democratic right by voting on the constitutional referendum. I voted yes for the constitution. Even though I have a lot of reservations about this constitution. The fact it had to be decided by the politicians on issues they had differences on (Mugabe, Tsvangirai and Mutambara), there are basic things good enough to endorse the constitution for that's why I voted for it. The best is on the limits of executive powers of the presidency (2 years limit). It's a good start. I hope it will pass through and we go for an election. We need to solve the economy of this country. We have been on the hang for far too long, and it's now time to sort it out, for the future of us and our kids

*

I have not been keeping regular diaries for I have been concentrating on proofing of *The Blame Game*. It's going well

*

Another issue I have been left hanging up on is on my relationships with Colleen and Kudzai. I have nothing much to say about Colleen, I am keeping my distance. I haven't seen Kudzai for some days, almost a week. A week ago we became deeply intimate, but without the sex of course. I am trying to get a head ahead of this relationship before I get involved sexually. I am still cut out emotionally…its only physical. I like her but I am still yet to get where I am falling in love with her. I am the relationship type of guy. I can't just have sex!

*

Another issue I would explore later is on happenings, miraculous things that are said to be happening all over the country, especially here in Chitungwiza. Some are saying it is the devil's work, some are saying it is God's work. I am not sure of any of this. I will explore them later

Wednesday 27 March 2013

Winter is creeping in. I can feel it in my bones and I have been hit by some flu bug, but I am getting better. When winter is seeping in it makes me feel restless. I am good though. A lot of things are happening, and I can't record them. Writing these diaries, I don't even know why I am writing them. Sometimes, in most cases, I can't really be able to shape stuff inside me into words, so I always feel it's not really me I am writing about. So I end up recording surfaces. I got another not great publishing deal with DIPPRESS, an US publisher, for my poetry collection, Playing to Love's Gallery, with poetry I wrote around 2009, when I was dealing with a broken relationship with Celine, in the diaries, It's Not About Me. The girl that really broke me. I am not going to write about her here. I have written so much about her before. That girl I keep trying to go back on and fix. The book will come out as an ebook, then later, print book. It's okay, it's always encouraging to get this kind of acknowledgement, even though it amounts to diddly. It shows I am keeping showing up. I hope I will have that one person who will enjoy it out there…that's the only basis of doing this. That one person is the difference.

*

There is always this Makandiwa thing in the air. Makandiwa is this prophetidiot (I don't know how else to capture him), who is making so called miracles here in Chitungwiza. Some months ago, it was said, he made some woman in his church to give birth to a kid when she had been fertilized for about three days. He said the woman had had sex with her ex hubby three days before and unbeknown to this woman, her egg had been fertilized, then he made her to give birth to a healthy kid. Having a kid in three days other than 9 months and the kid is growing well! I wonder a lot. Is that really a human being, that kid Makandiwa created with his miracles. Miracles are sleight of hand, duping things that humans perform on stupid and believing humans. I am still going to church. But even the miracles in the bible requires a kind of reading to accept them. God didn't even use his sperm to impregnate Maria in the bible, why? Going back to the Makandiwa's sleight of hand, what if this is a goblin, a half human, half spirit thing, and that, now it is human but would later become a monster it actually is. It's another mind-bending belief, believing that these things are goblins. Can a kid really be made in 3 days? Now Makandiwa, it is said, has challenged people to buy tickets for his Jesus walking on top of water miracle challenge, which is said is to take place on top of our biggest dam, Kariba Dam, on our northern border with Zambia. He wants to do the walking on top of the water, whatever for? It's a lot of people talking about this. For him it could be rivalry, came out of rivalry with another prophetidiot, Uerbert Angels, who is impressing his own church idiots with his own brand of miracles. The last time Angels told everyone in his congregation to check their wallets, cellphone accounts, bank accounts, and it is said they found money, more money they hadn't worked for. Just like manna, in people's pockets. So this is a game between these people which has blinded them and their followers. They now think religion is a game of miracles. I just can't get my head around it, maybe I need to gather more evidence

*

I am good. I think we have broken up with Kudzai. I am still not sure how I feel toward her. I don't even feel I need to patch up things with her. We have started talking to each other with Colleen, but it's still way out there before it can mean anything. She is cool. I think I am fighting against committing to one relationship with a girl. I like these little situationships. I could do that for a lifetime

*

And another moment the sun comes out, hot blistering late spring, early winter. The air is dry and hot, and some moment later, it hides in the clouds. A stubborn wind increases velocity and pelts things around, it's a cool mild wind, and these contrasts when seasons are changing irritates me. It percolates, my skins, my bones, my spirit...it makes me restless and bored.

*

These diaries are not working for me. I don't know what I am about in these diaries, but I don't seem to stop completely. So as long as I write something, once in a while, I will continue keeping them. The sky is almost completely draped in clouds now- cumuli-nimbus-status groups. Rain clouds- is it going to rain. We need the rains. It last rained 8 days ago- a heavy downpour out of nowhere. It has surprised us into thinking we are back in the thick of summer. This rainy season has been strange. One day it is cold, the cold of winter, and the whole of January it was raining almost every day, floods galore, broken bridges and gutted roads, gardens in river banks swept off, now it's generally dry. It is a drought year for a lot of people, not that it hasn't rained enough. It did but erratically so, crops lacked rains at critical points so the yield is going to be little, this year

*

The yes vote to the constitution triumphed, overwhelmingly-93percent. The first time it has happened in Zimbabwe. They have been 5 attempts at constitution construction in the history of Zimbabwe. Don't fret over the actual dates. In 1923 the white Rhodesians voted against a constitution crafted to allow Rhodesia's attempt to join the South African Union. In the 1969 there was also a constitution rejected against adoption of republicanism by the white people, and the other one was in 1979 for internal settlement to usher black rule, and in 2000 I was part of those who rejected another constitution making for land reform. And this one in 2013 is the first accepted by the Zimbabweans. I voted for it, not because I liked it. It's our only way forward, we need to get out of this quagmire and it's the only rope I can see. We had to make compromises. It's not what I would have wanted but it is what I could only have

Wednesday 10 April

I am not doing justice to these diaries. I am writing very little, generally. I haven't been writing much. I am more focused on promotion and marketing of my books. I am publishing two books this year and it's absorbing, but I am mostly sending my poetry to journals for publishing, and the responses are awesome. I think I have placed close to 50 pieces in over 20 magazines so far this year all over the world. I have also been focusing on trying artist residences. I got one in Colombia. I would like to try to get funding to get me there. I am a little excited. I would like to go to Colombia some day

*

Last week it was generally cold, very cold at night, but in the afternoon it's still warm autumn. The mornings are cold, winter is coming

*

I have started talking to Colleen again. Called her 2 days ago. She is receptive. I really like her. She is the girl I have liked for some time now and I am always willing to give it all my best but all depends on her willingness to explore this

*

This Colleen thing is impossible. She is impossible. Love is impossible

Wednesday 12 June 2013

It's been a long time since I have recorded something in these diaries. Pressure of other work. Its last night's jagged dream that makes me want to write this. I have since published *The Blame Game* and I think I have been having dreams that centres on the book. Infact maybe I am expressing my fears over my life through these dreams. The Blame Game is a hard hitting political book on Zimbabwe's political situation. It came out on 23 May, before that, I think a week before, I dreamt of Mugabe inspecting a guard of honour and I made fun of him. Some dark CIO figure ahead of me turned to look at me and told me to shut up. After that, when Mugabe had finished, he reclined into the nearby tent with this CIO guy to discuss my behavior. Sometime later, someone, the leader of the CIO came out of the tent and admonished someone who had been behind me to deal with me. I said I did nothing wrong that I was, infact, praising the old man. That he should leave me alone. They left me alone. A couple of days later I had another dream in which Mugabe was reading off a passage in my book, recognizing what I had written about him, though it was against him. He didn't seem angry. And in another slice of the dream, I am at our family home. I am trying and battling to put out fires that were all over our place. Eventually I got to this beautiful fruit and flower garden. Beautiful lawns. I had constructed it and I was boasting about it to my mother. It needed working on though, the garden was by our rural family home's gate and then I woke up

*

Monday and Tuesday there were two interviews about Zimbabwe The Blame Game and about me that came out from Kubatana.net…I think they are really good interviews although now I feel I talked too much, open my armpit too much in the interview about me. Some of the things I mentioned, I don't believe in them anymore

Saturday 27 April 2023

I had one of those craziest dreams. I have to record it. I haven't figured out where I was, but it was this crazy place at one time. There was a kitchen hand who doubled up as a cook. She was wearing an apron. I was coming into this place several times in this dream, obsessing about it. I was looking for someone. One time I saw someone I knew coming to this place and he offered a lift and I declined. Another moment it had crops in it, maize crop. At one time it was growing well, another time it had stunted. As I obsessed around this place, I had a feeling as if I was being chased, but I would hide well and see that no one was coming for me. Then some bug bite me by my forehead. It itches a bit so I scratch the place, then it starts dripping blood. At first it's not a lot so I am off to this place as it dries up, the wound that is. Then I am back again and as I am showing someone the wound, it starts dripping lots of blood into this field with maize. I am scared I am going to drain out every ounce of my blood, eventually it dries up. I am amazed by this as I come again to this place. I am looking for the blood, where I had dropped the blood, but I don't find any blood spots. I look and look, but I can't find it. In the dream I am thinking someone drunk up my blood. Then a bit later the place looks like my church place. It has several people I know from the church whom I have talked to yesterday in the afternoon through facebook. We are both complaining there is not enough food, eventually I get Sadza and sour milk, very little of it. I complain a bit, then I am given a cup. I am thinking it has milk so I pour it into the Sadza with that little sour milk, only to realize it is water I have added. I drink this mixture but do not eat the Sadza. Later, I am sited around the table. Some guys I know, Helen and Colleen, yes the Colleen I have written about in previous diaries is sited a bit of distance. She sees me and I make a disgusted with her face and she starts talking to Helen, making fun at me. Helen doesn't look at me, but they laugh. I am staring through Colleen. I don't have feelings for her. It's an oblique look I have for her. She still had issues with me but I am not interested anymore. Eventually I woke up, and it's the middle of the night. It difficult to go back to sleep

*

Helen was my person, a great friend. She died a few years later, in 2017

*

This Colleen character, I am no longer interested in her. If she is going to be there tomorrow, she hasn't been at the church for the last two weeks, I am going to ignore her. I don't have any feelings for her anymore. She has been abusing me, scolding me, cutting me on the phone, just being rude to me for a long time and I have had enough of it. I can't take the abuse anymore, so I have stopped.

Tuesday 8 July 2013

I have irrevocably fallen in love with Lilith kkkk. You all know that's not her name. For the larger part of 6 months we have been crushing into each other's lives without much effort on our part. It has been happening slowly, I think since mid-year last year when she separated from her former boyfriend Byron. But she took her time, dated another guy, I think she was trying to deal with a broken heart and get over Byron. I just kept close. She did keep me close too. She has always liked me, I think since we first met, Dec 2010. I didn't want her back then, to get into a relationship I wasn't ready for and also I wanted to get to know her as a friend. It was only this year, 17 Feb to be precise when I told her I was into her. She told me I was late for she was already seeing someone else. It bothered me for some time, but now I realize I still have feeling for her and I still had a chance, so I kept her close, haha by making her jealousy. I never saw the guy she said she was dating so it still meant I still have a chance, I took every opportunity to stay close to her, to hang with her and she liked it a lot. We got closer and closer, and for some time I thought we had drifted into a relationship but I had no courage to ask her about us. I knew at some point I had to talk to her or to continue drifting in but I had no courage to ask. So I asked playfully if she would be interested in seeing my sister as my girlfriend. She said no, she wasn't my girlfriend and she didn't want to see my family. It hurt me terribly for the rest of that week and when I saw her on the Sunday of 16 June, she wanted to hang with me but I ignored her. I guess she had had time to think. On Monday 17 June she sent a please call text message on my cell and I called her. We talked and she said she hadn't thought about it when I asked her and that's why she said no. she said I surprised her. That she likes me a lot. She was interested so that day we became a couple. It's not difficult to love her, she is a wonderful woman. I am glad and very happy. I am thinking of paying lobola for her and wed her next year. I am sure….

*

Of nothing, Fucking hell, it was another situationship!

Good morning my people

Good morning my people. Yes you and you and you…you are my people. I can also do the owning thing on you…after all you allow the priest, pastor, minister, governor, president to call you his/her people. Vanhu vedu tirikuda kuvapa minda nepfumbudza, whether they like it or not. Cherai makomba mvura yave pedyo kunaya says the clueless water spirit medium 'nehanda' president, you would almost think we are going to play nhodo (picking and dropping and taking over someone's stones adjacent to where you drop your last stone sport) in the 1 acre fields. The art is on targeting their holes that have more stones and hide your stones in the back lines that have their adjacent front lines devoid of nhodo… Hole after hole, after whole, after hoe, I mean that whole thing that cultivates… Man own, and then woman dispossess man in the home front. No wonder I used my people in the previous statement. And it's usually men who are in those positions of ownership. Woman are pushed into the kitchen, and boy she would own everything that resides in the home, including man.

Sorry, I stand corrected, I was stupid to think man own anything, rather its woman who own everything. My children, my husband, my kitchen, my plates and pans, "don't use my plates in the sideboard, I am keeping them for my Kugova nhaka, for my family. You want people to laugh at my corpse when I am dead, saying ndaiva rombe and couldn't even have good plates to feed people at my funeral." The way my people value and own the death horizon is something else. How the fuck does that matter, you will be dead. But you can't even ask them that question unless you want to be hit by more ownership diatribes like, "you should respect me, you are my son, you are my daughter, you came from my stomach, I carried you for 9 months. Usandisimudzira chivoice chako chinenge chigoritoto ichocho kufanana nababa vako. Your useless father, who leaves everything for me to do at home. Only coming from the sleeping hut and beer hall demanding I wait for him, to cook for him, to wash for him. You are my eggs…you do what I tell to do. Oh, I don't like your wife. You should have married Chengetai, not that thin wand light-skinned witch Shorai. She will bear lazy children for you. You are messing up our family colour pigmentation and dzinza. And if you don't marry soon, don't expect me to clean and cook for you douchebag, its time you should be cleaning and cooking for me. You are my son. I spend all my life taking care of you and now you are humburukwa, an old unmarried man who should be taking care of me. If you don't want to listen to what I am telling you to do go and start your own musha. Enda unoroorwa utongewo musha wako. Mumba hamungaite vakadzi vaviri or machongwe maviri. Oh you and your useless father think you own me. Ini Chihera ini chaiye tshek tschek puuu… He doesn't see I control him… Ini handijairirwe nemurume, this home belongs to me, kana asvotwa ngaabude, you see I am not going anywhere, ndofira pano. Pamusha pangu pano."

And man is assigned to the donor community position, I mean sperm donor…They don't even own what their sperm also create. And when you don't own your home you don't own the outside world too.

I hope you see you should be fine with me calling you my people. I fucking own you. Every human being wants to own another human being… the only animal that individually prospers through ownership of the next person, land, tree, country... Where did you buy the country you say you now own? We don't want refugees and illegal migrants in our country. Where the fuck did you think you came from. At one point you were a refugee and migrant too...except the Africans staying in Africa. Even those a few generations ago who were not even in this country now own the country versus those coming...when did you pay for it. You think I am joking, go to the UK now. The one who owns the Brishit and Northern Ireland, Shushi Sunak, hear him in his brishitness English telling migrants that they are not welcome to the country he didn't buy. The fucker was in Africa a generation ago, and India another generation behind. Trumpshit family came from Ireland a few generations away but he now owns the United States of Some American States...

I have to be sensitive to the rest of the Americas who have hated how the Americans own the word America as if it's the only country in the Americas. American dream, American sports (no one else gives a fuck about the world over. Don't get me started on their NBA world series....), American foreign policy interests, American way of doing things...all the while they are only just talking of the United States of Some American States. How come all the other American countries have their specific country names like Canada, Mehiko (I am doing the pronouncement thing on what you know as Mexico), Haiti, Cuba not golding, it's like the unnamed country they call South Africa, south direction of Africa, for fuck's sake Namibia, Swaziland (oh, they unowned this name and now call themselves Eswatini...I didn't say Esweating), Lesotho (the hoeing King's country),

Botswana (you pronounce it Motswana, meaning for the Tswana people, how about the Kalangas), are all in the south direction of Africa. You see I avoided the tinpot shaped country of stones to avoid the xenophobe in the direction south country.

Nelson Chamisa is his own Worst Enemy

He blames everyone else, his supporters blame everyone else, "it's because of Biti, it's because of Ncube, it's because of Sikhala who doesn't want to endorse Chamisa, it's because of the Mpidiots who don't want to resign, it's because of Tshabangu, and it's because of Mkwananzi who is a CIO, by the way who appointed Mkwananzi?

And another chorus, "it's because of ZANUPF, it's because of the government, it's because of the judiciary, it's because of ZEC, it's because of Mwonzora, it's because of Khupe…." It's really a long, long list of enemies

And the journalists in Zimbabwe cowers to him, publishing his accusations to kingdom come without thinking through what all that means.

A few years ago the old hulk at 1 Chancellor road used to use this same tactic, through his calculating wife and their G40 disciples, accusing everyone else: Mnangagwa, Mujuru, Chiwenga, Mutasa, Gumbo, Kaukonde…, have we forgotten the dressing down she inflicted on these before 17 November 2017?…and like Chamisa, Mugabe never blamed himself for the mess Zimbabwe had become.

The same tactic is now playing out with his anointed successor, time and again.

I have written extensive essays about opposition politics, so also ZANUPF in several of my books including among others, Zimbabwe: The Blame Game, Zimbabwe: The Urgency of Now, Zimbabwe: Beyond Robert Mugabe. I have criticized Mugabe, Mnangagwa, Chiwenga, Tsvangirai, Chamisa, Ncube, Biti… as a writer it's my job to say the truth as it is. Like it, don't like it…that's your call!

Chamisa is the problem.

First things first, Chamisa as I have noted before, is not a strategic thinker. Making him the president was the first mistake we made. He should have stayed as organizing Sec, a tactical leader, who pushes the masses, do the donkey work. He can't think four or five steps ahead. He rushes to do things without thinking them through, he has the sense of a god insect.

Any politician who thinks strategically knows a country and God are two different things. I am sure we know what's happening in Israel, where politicians there think they are entitled to Palestine because God said so thousands of years ago. I have no problem with people having their religion but God is not a landlord, the bible is not a constitution. The danger is when you think everyone else should subscribe to that view. Those who study religion would tell you people are moving away from Abrahamic religions, or the Abrahamic God. People are individualizing their spirituality. A lot of people hate the church with its manipulative abusive leaders, religion, God…even in Zimbabwe. So when you don't know how to separate the two, you are losing a good chunk who don't believe in your god, by continuing to preach about something they don't believe in. A politician is a politician, they work for the people, a pastor is a pastor, they work for God. I am sure we can all complain if our pastor, instead of preaching the gospel, focuses on talking about politics. Nelson thinks he sits between the people and God and controls God to only mean what he wants and that only he is entitled to lead the opposition.

He and only he is anointed to lead the opposition, and Zimbabwe.

In 2014 during the MDC T congress I am sure all those who follow politics of the opposition know Chamisa had extruded every opposition to the secretary general position, after Biti had left to form his own party. He had manipulated the structures to vote for him. I will use speculation here, they say Morgan got scared of how Chamisa had rocked things around to fit to his purposes, to ultimately kick Tsvangirai to the carb not so long into the future, so they said Tsvangirai supported Mwonzora's bid at the 11th hour. Mwonzora had only one province, Manicaland, that had endorsed him, Chamisa had all the other provinces. But through whatever machinations in the MDC's council, Mwonzora beat Chamisa to the throne. Those who had endorsed Chamisa voted for Mwonzora...so thus begun the fight between the two. But Tsvangirai was afraid he would lose Chamisa to Biti, so he appointed him and Mudzuri to some smaller compensatory positions. Checkmate! And eventually he found his way into assisting the president when Tsvangirai was ill. And as Tsvangirai lie in comatose, barely alive...we all know of the tweet that made Chamisa, all of a sudden, the MDC T president. And with his hooligans who almost burned Mwonzora and Khupe alive at Tsvangirai's funeral and the colluding executive members, they ring fenced the presidency. He assumed the presidency illegally. Everyone with a little bit of brain knew it was just a matter of time before someone threw the spanners at him in the courts. And someone did. He lost the presidency. Can I blame the courts? No, I can't. The MDC's constitution was clear, only the deputy president elected at previous Congress had the right to take over in case the president is dead or incapacitated. Anyone taking that case to court, any court in the world, he would have won. They would have made the same decision. Because the constitution was clear. It doesn't matter there was a tweet, it didn't matter Tsvangirai had previously appointed him as his assistant...I don't need to explain the difference between assistant to president and deputy president...those are totally different positions. The minister who works in Mnangagwa's office is an assistant to Mnangagwa who is the president...but he is never the deputy president. Chiwenga and Mohadi are the deputy presidents. So it was simple, Khupe should have taken over, and later convened a congress to elect a substantial president. But politics is politics, a good part of the MDCT executive supported Chamisa because they didn't have faith in Khupe wining against Mnangagwa in 2018. But legal is legal. The courts did their work.

Chamisa still felt he was a godhood who was being denied what he was entitled to, so he left MDCT and sneaked into MDC Alliance as its president, but as I noted law is law, politics is politics. MDC alliance had been created by Tsvangirai's MDCT, Biti's PDP, and Ncube's MDCN before Tsvangirai's demise…it only meant the recognized by law leadership of MDC T party was going to head MDC alliance (that was their agreement when they formed MDC Alliance). The court's decision meant all MPs who were representing MDC Alliance in the election were answerable to the MDCT executive endorsed by the court's judgment. So Khupe (Acting president) and Mwonzora (Sec Gen) were the recognized leaders of MDC Alliance. It was a fair judgment, following the constitution of the MDCT and MDC Alliance. No one took the MDCT away from Chamisa. No one took the MDC Alliance from him. It wasn't his to begin with.

But he soldiered on, buoyed by his hooligans and supporters and went to an election, the Gweru congress of 2019. Here is how the god got his way around. He kicked most of the MDCT leadership that supported Mwonzora, had Mwonzora harassed by his hooligans. At one time Mwonzora was barred from coming to the MDC's offices for meetings by these hooligans, Mudzuru was chased around, Khupe was abused to the level I felt really, really sick. They stifled Mwonzora and camp who wanted the constitutional route followed, called him all sorts of names, called him the traitor because he wasn't kneeling to their god. All the provinces endorsed Chamisa with the exception of the proverbial Manicaland, which Mwonzora still could control. So he did the next trick available, talked to Mwonzora, promised to support him in his bid for SG position in turn Mwonzora endorsed Chamisa for presidency thus Manicaland endorsed him too…but at the congress which was held clandestinely, sometimes in the middle of the night, he did his usual trick he later came to do on Biti in 2023. He supported and pushed for Hwende and other young student-politics guns, and extruded Mwonzora out of the executive and humiliated him the same way Tsvangirai had done to him in 2014 by offering him a minor position.

And then the withdrawals of MPs begun, it was tit for tat. It's Chamisa who had thrown Mwonzora under the bus, so Mwonzora and Khupe used the constitutional route to withdraw MPS…and the heat got to be too much for Chamisa so he ran out and formed CCC.

Him, and a few MDCTs and former PDP and MDCN leaders who had been elected at Gweru congress parted ways with Mwonzora and created a new organization with this MDC Alliance leadership in control. Chamisa, as you can see, had been abused by the constitutions that kept derailing him from taking over his anointed position. So he refused to have a constitution for CCC, he demoted everyone he had formed the CCC with. He refused to have structures, membership cards... Willy-nilly appointed those he wanted to use, eg Mkwananzi.

He was the sole leader. He was the constitution, he was the only member, he was the sec general, he was the treasurer....it was his thing. Nothing, no structure was going to deny him being the president he was anointed for this time. He went to the election that disorganized in August 2023 and lost it. CCC won over a third of the seats which was commendable. But law is law, it only works with law and history (meetings). If you are the president of a party that has MPs, supporters, a party that represent the interests of a chunk of the population, was registered for elections...there has to be an organ that made you president. Him competing as the face of CCC is not an election or endorsement. He is just the face. Lol, I am not going to dwell on his face that Tshabangu now claims he owns. I might be accused of usurping Tshabangu's rights to Chamisa's face. That level of idiocy is something else that requires other creative crafts to depict. It's a congress (meeting) that elects leadership. A party can chose someone to represent them in any election and still have a different substantial president of the party. Recall Mutambara/Ncube situation a few years back. There was no constitution (for me to be a Zimbabwean I am recognized through the constitution of Zimbabwe, that's where I get my rights as a citizen of Zimbabwe.) CCC had no constitution, no membership cards to show who is part of the group and who is not, no structures...all those only resided in the head of Nelson Chamisa. And imagine someone complaining that the judiciary voted against Chamisa, Tshabangu wasn't a CCC member? Which constitution or membership cards in the CCC that said that? Does the president know all the 1.9 million voters who voted for him by head, so that he could say Tshabangu wasn't part of the CCC? If he endorsed himself as the president, why shouldn't anyone else claim any other position in the party? There was no congress that elected him. There was no constitution that recognized him, there were no structures and membership cards. It was simply his word against that of Tshabangu, and why should his word have taken preponderance in the judges' decisions? The judgment simply means what it means, anyone in Zimbabwe can stand up and say they are the SG, Treasurer, president, Deputy etc… of CCC. And the withdrawals continued. So he couldn't stand the heat and left accusing everyone else of this and that. Despite the fact that he is on record saying having a party without all these was his only way to avoid infiltration, to secure the people's vote… he left,

Continuing his history of wanting his and his way only. Or leaving…

Chamisa is a pretentious liar.

I am not going to waste time repeating his fanciful worlds of Spaghetti roads crisscrossing cities and villages in Zimbabwe, bullet trains bulleting through the eastern highlands' mountains hungering for the flatter Mashonaland valleys, and the surreptitious Gutu's village Airports. Milk and honey flowing in the sewage streams that houses the sewages now as they pour into Hunyani River, oh you know that fantastical stuff of heavenly bodings in bible people's minds. I am going to stay practical!

Before he went into the elections last year I am one of those who supported absconding the elections because of the reforms that needed to be done (overdue since they were agreed to during GNU) even post-August 2018 Army killings recommendations by the commission of inquiry headed by Monthlane asked for Security sector reforms. Without the reforms what was the reason to go to an election everyone else knew was lopsided in favour of the ruling party? If you go to an election knowing the limitations and imbalances, you have endorsed those limitations and imbalances, you have no reason to complain afterwards.

He lied he knew how to protect our vote, that never again shall ZANUPF steal our vote. Post 2018 election he had refused to endorse the elections because ZANUPF had stolen the election from him. He dismally failed to prove before the courts how ZANUPF had stolen the vote because he didn't have the infamous V11 forms for the areas he was contesting, after failing to field agents there. He expected ZEC to afford him the evidence. He failed to do his job as leader to make sure agents were fielded in the said areas (about 50 constituencies), so he wanted the court to use speculations and a few lawyerly jargon from Thabane Mpofu, his lawyer, to decide in favour of him. It was just a pathetic and desperate demonstration. The court did their job.

Please note, I am not saying our judiciary is without blame. Take in case Job Shikala's case where he was denied his constitutional right by the courts for bail. He spent almost 2 years in remand, locked for a small crime that his core-accused were given bail for, for no reason other than to persecute him. And after two years they gave him a sentence of two years in jail, suspended. See how it doesn't make sense, the guy had already done two years, so what are they suspending....the conditions tells it all...he is not supposed to commit another crime like the one he was sentenced for in the next 2 years ...if he did then he will serve those two years suspended plus the new sentence. They have corralled him for the next two years. But knowing our Job, he will be back in the court before the magistrate disrobed her magisterial gown. So our judiciary isn't free by a hoot. But in these cases they followed the law, maybe knowing they were on the right side of it with the politicos in ZANUPF.

Five years later Chamisa decided to go to another election without agents in at least 2500 polling booths out of 12374 (in 2018 it was 513 out of 10985 polling stations). You see the situation is even worse. Before the election results were announced he had already decided his position. It was only him winning the election or the election is stolen. And he stuck to his guns, created all sorts of crazy theories as usual. Come the deadline date to send the case to the courts, he still didn't have V11 forms as I noted above in over 2500 places. He knew it was useless going to the courts that had told him to produce V11s in 2018 and he had failed, so he did his usual preening around diplomatic circles and newspapers that entertain him as usual.

And now we are back to square one. The opposition is fractured almost to beyond repair. He is blaming everyone else. He wants to form another structureless outfit and people are being terrorized by his hooligans online to support and follow him and only him. He is the little god of Zimbabwe politics.

It is high time Zimbabweans, the majority of whom are not members of any of these political parties, should take a breather, sit down and ask themselves hard questions. Do we need to keep following these shenanigans (lol, sorry Mr Deputy president Chiwenga, it's your word, I know) or start demanding these politicians to focus on the real issues we are facing (unemployment, service delivery, skyrocketing cost of living, insane monetary regime, inflation, corruption, mismanagement of the economy, sanctions). Chamisa cannot sort Zimbabwe alone, it's obvious. If you still think he can like his hooligans do, you need to have your mind examined. Because there is nothing that can stop him from chickening away after winning in 2028 and run out, accusing everyone else but himself of failure to deliver, that is if he wins it to begin with. Will he win? No, I don't see it. He has burned too many bridges, no sane person wants to follow him anymore. He needs to come back to the middle, work with all opposition politicians in Zimbabwe as partners, not his toy soldiers he uses, or maybe take a breather from politics, take some time away to reflect and learn his mistakes.

Who wants to invest thousands of dollars to campaign to be an MP under someone who if he doesn't find his way around a difficult situation, would ask them to recuse themselves from the jobs they got after pouring thousands of their sweat into. Any politician in CCC knows going with Chamisa and only Chamisa chete chete (CCC) strategy, post 2028 it would be the same cry song, so why not finish their terms now and move on with their lives if they fail to get elected in 2028. At least they would have recouped their outlay. Being an MP is a job like any other job. You work to get paid. You need to provide for your families. You need to be motivated in order to deliver. Only someone with godhood noises in their heads expect politicians to only be worried about going to heaven like servers who serve without pay in the church. So you see for Chamisa these are his disciples. It's his church he is going to form again. Everyone has to obey him and him only because he is the only one with the keys to heaven. In an interview with Studio 7 he said,

"People make the mistake of thinking that I do things as an individual. No, there are forces, you know, I have one chief advisor. People will say 'who is his advisor?' The holy spirit is the powerful advisor for each and every human being..."

As clear as a day is out, it's a cult and toxic to the hilt. Like ZANUPF or the government of Zimbabwe, the CCC doesn't care about the democratic process they attack ZANUPF for not practicing. The

CCC or opposition is as worse as ZANUPF when it comes to service delivery in the urban areas they control. Of course they have excuses why they have failed to deliver for over 20 years. It's ZANUPF to blame. For Chamisa, it's only himself whom he will listen to, or the Holy Spirit, or the God he dangerously abuses every day. You might as well go and argue with your ancestors, Chamisa is always right and everyone else who is against him is the traitor. He is the god of Zimbabwe's politics.

I stopped voting in 2013 with thousands others fatigued by our politics, I always voted for opposition. In 2018 he lost thousands who loved Mwonzora and Khupe, some stopped voting altogether like me. Now he has lost thousands who support each and every individual MP who would stick with CCC and a lot more will stop through fatigue and our incredibly impossible situation we have. And I can bet my last dollar, come hell come thunder, he will never win in 2028. His support will go down by some thousands like what happened last year. He is his worst enemy. Chamisa is to blame for his problems.

THE EVIDENCE OF THINGS SAID:

Diaries (2014-2015)

Monday, December 1, 2014

PHEW!!! I don't even know where to start with these diaries, what they will be addressing, why I should write them, keep them, what path they would take, why continue with diarising when in the last diaries I could not do a lot of these, got bored, stopped altogether way before the endpoint of my diary series. I have toyed with titles and have returned often to one title, but I don't even know why that title and whether I should take it as the title of these diaries. The last diaries I wanted to toy with the title- *Gathering Evidence*, but I still feel I didn't do well by it. This cycle will toy around THE EVIDENCE OF THINGS SAID, or is it unsaid, and it's obvious unsaid is the best title, because by writing them then I am saying those things unsaid. But I want to work with those that were said to highlight those unsaid, that's why I decided on THE EVIDENCE OF THINGS SAID as the title. Said and unsaid, I feel are shifting states of expression for each might work with the other, or precipitates into the each other. I tank it. But it's very clear I am still interested in evidence…, I still don't know what evidence, though!

****

Today is a cloudy, cool day (these are facts, evidence of this day) it seems the clouds are full of rains but it hasn't been letting out rains for days. It has been hot the last two weeks and now it has cooled down. I need the rains. By now I think you all know I love rain. I want it so bad that it rains. But it seems it has been raining up there in the clouds without a drop sneaking past the clouds to cool me down

****

I am listening to Enya's music on the album, *Paint the Sky with Stars*, beautiful music…that's not even the term for it, man. This is music, music, music…too good to be described with words. I feel like if I could just ask me to help her paint the sky with stars I will never be able to stop myself from doing that for the rest of my life. I tend to listen to her music to cool down, especially when I am high-strung, too busy, too stressed, too impatient, feeling too good…and it softens all these down, and soften my insides, too

****

Am I in love, hahahaha, that perennial situation is with me? I am always thinking I am in love…but why. I don't know. Do I want to be in love, maybe it's a constant thing with me. I am always thinking I am starting out something with someone, holding onto someone, but it never really stays. I am writing poetry, stories, tales, plays, essays, novels, writing, writing, always writing. Sometimes I feel overwhelmed in the words I have put pen to. Are these my thoughts, what is me in these words? If they are all really me, then what's me now left secret, to me, something I haven't shared with anyone. A person can have all these words, these thoughts, send them out there into the world, my oh my, I sometimes feel like just stopping this bleeding, clam up and do something else, be somewhere else. Sometimes I wish I was an accountant, a mathematician, a statistician, I didn't have to use words. I don't have to leave behind a part of me that someone out into the future will read and call that me. $1+1=2$, and it will remain like that and it would never belong to the statistician, accountant or mathematician, but these words, these thoughts will always belong to me, will shape into what the future will judge me for, will know me by. Being somewhere is what I really want to do. I have stayed here for far too long now. Never thought I will be around here longer than I have been. I want out now, so badly. I have tried to leave before but I didn't have enough conviction to do so. Now I think I really want out of this bloody hell hole. I said I have been writing too many words, and to stop doing that I have tried other art fields- photography, which I started being serious about somewhere last year. And I have been publishing a lot of photography this year. I did start doing music and sound art last year too, and I have been publishing a lot of that too, and working on some more compositions. I want to learn some instruments, compose on these instruments, like the mbira, violin, viola, cello, and guitar…those are my favourite instruments. About midyear I started drawing too, and I have been drawing. Lately I have started on collagen and poetry translations, which I will be exploring too. I also do video work too but haven't focused on it that much. Thus I am panning out to be a multidisciplinary artist I have also thought I can be. My attitude about art is experimentation, collaboration ("as the slim condition of possibility"), being open to new things or to just newness, thus I will keep exploring all these art forms and fields more and more.

******

This year I have also completed my twentieth year as a writer, for I started in 1994, somewhere in the middle of that year , I don't remember the actual date in 1994, thus I have also been thinking of a retrospect of some sort, looking back to where I came from, going back there. Maybe I will create a complete works in one of the genres I started with in 1994, most likely poetry for I have been writing poetry constantly since 1994 and have in excess of 400 poems to date, which is significant.

****

2.59 pm. I have just had lunch- Sadza with pumpkin leaves. Summer months I eat a lot of greens and summer weeds.

****

I am constantly planning on what I am working on. Checked whether there is anything more I can add to the novel, A DARK ENERGY. Yes the novel I have noted in my dairy circle, ITS NOT ABOUT ME (2010-2011), and I was writing it back then. Have since finished it and it has been with Zach Oliver's Aignos publishing co. Not a lot of progress about it for the past 2 years he has been with it. I was almost plucking it off his hands a couple of months ago, but I thought I should give him time, and I should have a look at it as he asked me to do again. There is not much change I can make to the storyline and narrative, but may change the presentation, and soften it a bit. Now I feel I can't do anything to it anymore, thus if he expresses reservations on it again, then I will pluck it off. It's frustrating me. I have been patient because we have worked well together on KEYS IN THE RIVER, when he was still the chief editor at Savant Books.

****

I wrote a poem in the morning whilst I was doing chores like watering the garden, cooking…, entitled *Body*. Its part of the collection I have just started, WHEN ESCAPE BECOMES THE ONLY LOVER, still at the legs level, but it will pan out into a huge book, I know.

******

I like this girl- incredibly *like* her. She is super-fun, confident, sweet, beautiful, and incredibly open. I can talk to her and forget where I am. I want to keep talking to her, fighting with her, agreeing and disagreeing with her, holding her in… my arms. I don't know why. She is going through a heartbreak, recently ended her relationship with her boyfriend. I am friends with both. She discovered a drawer-full of the boyfriend's dirty, which I knew though about, and hadn't told her. She is not really pleased with me now that I kept it away from her. I couldn't tell her all that. I don't tell. It's none of my business. I am glad she discovered that on her own and it's her decision to call off the relationship.

Wednesday 3 December 2014.

Yesterday I wanted to write something but failed, I had a hectic day. I am making last edits for my nonfiction book *Zimbabwe: The Urgency of Now*. I wrote it between January and April this year, and it's now coming out from Langaa RPCIG, my publisher of *Zimbabwe: The Blame Game*. The Urgency of Now is a follow up to The Blame Game…, focusing on Zimbabwe in the post-power sharing period, the 2013 elections, and post these elections, too. It is a more focused book as compared to The Blame Game, and bends more to the academic genre, the task of which has been trying for me, to follow academic rules. But I have to make an effort towards making it appeal to the academic establishment, which, even though The Blame Game was a bit unstructured, it has appealed to the academic establishment quiet well as it invades world-class University libraries and public libraries. So I will be focusing on this market with this new text. Most likely it will come out beginning of next year. I am a bit frustrated and strained.

******

I am broke, but it's something I have always dealt with well. I know I will be okay, but still broke. Writing or maybe the arts is a thankless activity, but I hope someday I will get something out of it. Not that I write for the money. I will still write even if I am never going to get something substantial from it. Writing is breathing to me. I can't stop breathing.

It's sunny, hot summer day, and it didn't rain and the skies are now clear of clouds as if it never thought of crying, a couple of days ago. Why do I feel bereft and lost? I think it has always been a perpetual feeling with me. I don't feel I belong to anything, to anyone. Yes, I don't belong to anyone. I am lonely but busy, otherwise I was going to be more bereft and lost, frustrated. Does frustration act as my muse? I have often thought I write well when I am not frustrated. I don't know. Sometimes I do write well under frustration.

******

I am drawing, writing poetry, stories, diaries, plays etc..., photographing things, making sound art, but why am I doing all these rather than to stick with writing alone. Why all this lot, yet I can't stop. It keeps me so much busy and away from my think-tank of a mind. Generally I am more fulfilled as an artist, even though as a person I am less so.

******

Why is it that when one grows older they tend to feel a little more detached with everything, yet they should be a close feeling with things due to their familiarity. I feel I don't love, feel, have the same fouled up beautiful emotions and feelings over a lot of things. Some things or people I don't feel anything for yet I had felt so much more for, in the past. Where is that hot blood I used to have in my system? Have I been dying slowly, emotionally. I know physically I am dying slowly now, with my eyes on the forefront on this race to death, they don't see much anymore. It might be a very long road to the actual death. I want it long so that I might in the future find that feeling, hot feeling I had with things or some people. I know someone out there is telling me that there is no time, be whatever you want to be now, feel those things now for you might die tomorrow. I know that. I don't care. But I also believe the hoping for something better in life, in tomorrow, drives us to keep trying, and one can deal themselves a great hand if they believe there is always a chance, a hope for the best tomorrow. It is what drives us to keep trying, so I need this tomorrow, even though I know it's not guaranteed to me.

****

I am angry with myself, or with some girls who make me angry with myself, especially when they say or show that they love me and yet I want to love them back and get the thing off, but I don't have it in me to do so. It makes me angry with myself. I know their love is inadequate for me. Most of these days I just ignore them; I need a stronger love. Something that would stop me, enslave me, halt me. I can't seem to find that love

Wednesday 10 December 2014.

I need to take time on these diaries. I have been incredibly too busy processing applications for university studies next year. I am focusing on getting a place next year in the UK or USA universities, and maybe do that masters in creative writing that I have vacillated on for years. I remember I first applied for this degree in 2009 at Hull University; got it but I couldn't take it due to no finances for study. Up to now, I think I haven't taken it mostly due to failure of procuring funding. Even though deep down I also think this degree is of no use to me, I might take the chance given. This year I would try to look for financing seriously, or apply at universities that offer full funding like Iowa, Cornel, East Anglia

Saturday 13 December 2014.

I am not in a comfortable place with myself. I feel restless, baddish sort of, the energy around me is a bit dark, but I try to keep myself close to myself, not to overact at others. It has been a very funny summer so far. It is not raining. The skies, in the morning are always laden with heavy rainy clouds but it rains up there in the skies. Sometimes it's so cold you would almost think its winter, and then in the afternoons the skies clear up and it gets hotter. This year the change has been significant. I couldn't sleep well last night. This summer there are too many mosquitoes. They were all over me trying to bite me. I spent the night trying to wade these off me; also there was just this restlessness around me. Maybe it has something to do with a girl I like who has not been behaving well towards me. I don't want to talk about her, until there is really something solid to talk about her. I am tired of these on and off girls, and my on and off into love life. Another thing I don't want to focus on these diaries is the political situation in Zimbabwe because of its on and offish way about them. It's like a soap opera, so I have tried not to follow it that much or write about it.

In short the MDC had its congress in October, and retained Tsvangirai on the helm, Douglas Mwonzora as the sec general. It's pretty much people loyal to Tsvangirai, people without open ambitions for his position who made the list, with rivals like Nelson

Chamisa biting the dust. I think it's a let's wait and see leadership they created, maybe until we get to an election. There is nothing interesting to write home about this leadership in the MDC. Then the ZANU-PF had an explosive congress, last week. It started with Grace Mugabe's (Robert Mugabe's wife) bitchy (sorry for the use of this expression, but if it means something, then that's exactly how she behaved) confrontation, head on style when she lambasted everyone in the ZANU-PF who fought against the president. She did it in a way never before seen or witnessed in Zimbabwe (even Mugabe lashing at Tsvangirai over the years was kid's stuff as compared to Grace's). She let rip and she focused the party towards where she wanted it to go (or where Robert Mugabe wanted it to go). In the process Grace got her PHD she never worked for at University of Zimbabwe, and the women affairs secretariat in the ZANU-PF. She made the party to push off most of its senior leaders (Mujuru in particular was stripped of her vice presidency by a colluding Mugabe), and others like Ray Kaukonde, Temba Mliswa, Didymus Mutasa, Jabulani Sibanda, Dzikamai Mavhaire, Nicholas Goche, Olivia Muchena, and the list is endless, lost their positions through this engineered push by Grace. Most of those involved in the wiki leaks debacle of a year or so ago were pushed out, so it seems the machinery waited for an opportune time to deal with those and Grace drives this machinery now. She aired, pointed, poked, raged, spat, like a crazy house wife every of these, especially the vice president, Mujuru. There were pushed out with the collusion and trickery use of Grace's by Mnangagwa's camp which now controls the ZANU-PF and Mnangagwa was given the vice president position he has coveted for years and is now the anointed successor of Mugabe. At least he is near Mugabe and can influence for successorship from close at hand but you can't rule out other eventualities in the ZANU-PF. It's possible to see Grace Mugabe adorning the winning jersey in 2018, but the most likely is we will have our old man in the wheelbarrow, being wheeled to the voting station, still competing for the leadership position in 2018, as long as he can still control his flock, which he has always been able to do, robotically. That's why I said the politics in Zimbabwe is boring because I don't even see ZANU-PF loosing 2018, not to Tsvangirai on his own, not to Mujuru on her own, not to the Lovemore Madhukus, Welshman Ncubes, Tendai Bitis, Simba Makonis of Zimbabwe, no…only, as I noted in *Zimbabwe: The Urgency of Now*, if all these were to unite into one opposition party, which I don't see them doing because these oppositions leaders are too egotistical, selfish and money-mongering idiots. So as long as Mugabe is there he will win it (whether through stealing or actually winning it by fair means) It is so tense, even a war is not just a far off thing. War is the only thing that can undo ZANU-PF. Grace broke the party down, but still it didn't die. The talk all over the country is now whether Mujuru is going to raise up and confront her humiliations or if she is going to fight quietly in the ZANU-PF, until she gets back into top leadership. Is she leaving the ZANU-PF to create a party of her own with the bulk of her followers and upenders noted above? Is she joining the opposition front with the MDCs. We can only speculate now.

Friday 18 December 2014

It has been raining for 4 plus days now, wonderful rainfall, the rains I love, soft sneezing from the skies. I feel great when it rains

*

I had my first maize cob from the garden patch I planted in August. Good great food. Had the maize with tea in the morning. In the afternoon I had Sadza with Malawian mowa relish, summer greens). I love these summer weeds. But I do constantly have this meal for I have always dried excess of these weeds for winter months when they will be little or none in the fields

*

My patch of land opposite St Mary secondary school grounds has a good cropping of maize, groundnuts, roundnuts, pumpkin, cowpeas, wild cowpeas (Nyembwe), mowa, black jack, sweet potatoes etc

*

I have been concentration on applications for university for next year. I had completed Cornell application but the friends (Zach and Jennie Oliver) I had hoped will help me with application fee (100 dollars, could not transfer it in time so I lost out. So yesterday I started on Syracuse university- to long, about 15 pages, frustrating American university entry application procedures are too cumbersome, too much paper, too much to fill up as compared to British universities. I am trying both British and American, and my favorite are British universities because it takes only a year to do a masters there than 2 or 3 years in American Universities. I don't like the classroom, so any less is favourable by me. What do they want to teach about, about writing, that I don't know or already do?

Tuesdays 23 Dec 2014

I have to shake it off, these situationships, these love stunted excursions. I discovered the girl I was beginning to like is getting married next April. I have to let it go. Who, Tambu…but she was lying

*

It's been shit since yesterday when she told me that. I feel grated. I am dealing with much on my plate. I am getting stuck, it's so difficult completing my university application, as I feel stunted, still trying to figure out how to pay for application fee for Iowa. I had to forgo Cornell as noted in previous diary because Zach failed to pay for me in time. He has been silent, not replying my follow up letters about it. I might have to figure out how to do it if from this end

Thursday 25 December 2014

Today is Xmas day

Oh, hell whatever!

My father has just called at 12.50 pm, that's a positive maybe. It's not such a bad day as such. I am a bit bored and unhinged

*

Unhinged because I am dealing with my feelings of Tambu. I am beginning to realize I like her a lot than I thought. Don't we always do that the more the love interest is not available?

*

But I will be fine

Friday 26 December 2014

I am still trying but I don't know if I have to go all the way in, in trying to win Tambu, or just continue letting her go

*

I am not having a great Xmas holiday. I haven't had a great one for ages. Maybe it comes with growing up, letting things go, letting go of Childhood fantasies, knowing every day is no different from the next or previous, thinking this is pretty much my life

*

12.57, it's raining. It has been very hot in the mornings and now it has cooled with the rains, sudden rains. You do expect them in the summers though. Most likely it has always rained on the 25th or 26th. Yesterday it didn't, today it is

*

I am listening to rock and pop music. There is this amazing song, *Show me Heaven by Maria Mckee* on the repeat, been blasting it for months, since I got the song in September. I have no words for how I like it

Monday 29 December 2014

We are two days off 2015, and I am writing this diary at 16.20, afternoon. It's very hot, yet yesterday it rained cats and dogs, and I was slogged to hell coming from church youth activities. I keep asking myself, am I still a youth? I am 41

*

I don't think so, but I can't seem to stop going there. It is something I have done since 1998, at this church, infact a lot earlier, about 1984/5 but it was in Nyanga back then

*

But in Chitungwiza it has been regular since 1998, I have seen it all, but there is still that attachment to that, even though everything about me protests against it

*

Would I ever stop, maybe if I marry soon. Which is a big maybe

*

But I am beginning to have difficulty connecting with the youngsters who are youths of today in my grouping. We are worlds apart and I feel lost

*

Maybe I should just make a clean break. Set on with my life without that

*

An hour ago I was talking to a distant relative who has her relationship with her abusive, a drunk husband. She is thinking of leaving him. Their relationships has hit the rocks, after another beating and abuse from him. The husband doesn't take care of the wife, the kids or anyone else but himself, not really- of his beers, smoke, drugs etc. The wife of Cain

*

It guts me to see her suffering and wonder why some man marry when they are not mature enough to sustain a serious and balanced marriage. The man is emotionally immature. Would he ever grow? I doubt it!

*

She is saying this time when she leaves him, she won't return this time. It's painful to realize that she is not convinced she should be leaving this thug again. She seems helpless in this maze of abuse, beatings etc. She left some years ago when she couldn't take it anymore. She had one kid then, but she returned back and the husband saddled her with another kid. Now she is thinking of leaving him again

*

I doubt she will. There is not enough conviction. Maybe she will

*

And that hubby doesn't abuse the wife only. Everyone at this home is always complaining about him, including his own mother, nieces and brother

*

His nieces grew up under this abuse system and they are not doing well; abortions, escapades, naughtiness, and the youngest niece has just eloped with a boyfriend who is already married. She is barely 16 and already 8 months pregnant, and a wife. It's sad. I am told she is refusing to return home, afraid of the abuse and shame, even sexual abuse by this lout

Wednesday 7 January 2015

7 days into the new year, and I hadn't found some time to spare on the diaries. I am just going to put a note down today

*

I am incredibly busy, and tired. I am letting her go and moving on. Not much in this of that Tambu girl

*

There is this buddy girl, Munashe I do talk to a lot. Ok, I am attracted to her. Have been for a years now but she was with someone. Now she is single

*

We have drifted terribly crazy close each other. I don't know what will become of it, but I will have to try it

Friday 13 March 2015

You think I didn't try, I did. I got burned again. We have drifted badly with Munashe

*

If I love something, if I want something I try to get it, that's me

Friday 8 May 2015

And I got it this time. We have drifted back into each other's good graces. We are dating, but it's still fragile, difficult to understand. On my side I know I want this, maybe more than I have been lately. I feel like I am on a cusp of something. She is a cute sweet girl. I love her

*

I am working across several levels and genres, forms, disciplines, so my world is incredible. Sometimes I feel I am lost, just drifting from one project that needs to be done there and then to the next that needs to be done there and then

*

A biggest part of the year has been taken in writing new works but other stuff, mentoring writers in Writivism Uganda project, pushing for publication of my old material, editing, proofing, letters to editors and publishers, really most of my major manuscripts might get published this year. I am chasing at least 5 books publication. I have one already out, a nonfiction book Zimbabwe The Blame Game from Langaa, and I am midway editing two books earmarked for publication by Langaa too, *Revolution: Struggle poems* and *Finding a way home* (fictions). Another full length novel, *A Dark Energy* we are midway editing with Zach Oliver who wants to publish it under his new label, Aignos Publishing. I am also compiling a collection of scholarly essays with Professor Munyaradzi Mawere of Great Zimbabwe University.

*

I am trying to adapt to the cold we are now blanketed in as we dip into winter season. I feel cold and frozen in my brains. I am hardly writing even though sometimes I get time to. I am frozen.

Monday 10 August 2015

I have to unfocus off these affairs for me to constantly record something in the diaries. That world of relationships of mine is making no sense to me anymore, so trying to follow these is time wasting

*

I think it's difficult trying to figure the state of things in Zimbabwe. It doesn't make sense politically, emotionally, economically, things are getting harder by day by day. You get the sense of suffocating, compressed feeling into a grave you might never come out from. I think I have to refuse being buried in this grave

*

A week ago I was really down, so lonely, I thought of disbanding Chitungwiza for my rural home Nyanga, where my parents stay. It is so hard. I thought I could just leave everything and go back to where it all begun for me, maybe I could find a fresh perspective, but the feeling has passed away

*

I will fight some more. I will write more. I am going to spend some time on these diaries, all the way until end of year. I hope I will be a bit successful in this cycle than the previous one

*

Winters are difficult times for me. Generally my output goes down in winter. I am temptous, lazy, brooding, cold, frozen in winter. I think I only wrote one piece since winter descended like a fucking thief. *Towards the United States of Africa, concepts, issues and methodologies*, which I am co-writing with Mawere for our book project we are editors to, *Democracy, Good Governance and Development in Africa, Towards a sustainable in growth in Africa*…just a rough title. We will decide on the final topic later. We have invited professors, doctors, academics all over Africa and African Diaspora to be contributors. We are in the last month of the call

*

I have since published 3 books but have withdrawn one of which, Graph of Love. The editor/publisher laterally pissed over and defecated on my poems and I complained. The publisher, Tatenda Munyuki couldn't reply to my complains and decided to call it quits. I accepted it. I couldn't accept what he had done to my poems, the way he went around his business is uncouth too

*

15.30, I just came from the internet café. Passed through Zengeza Shopping centre, the free market area. Nobody is there trading, they are at the grounds for heroes celebrations, forcefully taken there to show appreciation of our heroes.

*

I think I am now healed. Looking forward to moving on with my life without Munashe. For the past months have been hell. Now, I am ok. Evidence is what you are looking for. Check how my diaries died down from May up until today. You think it was the winter's cold only that made me clammed up. Nope. The lack of these diaries have her to thank her. I think I went through some form of depression, but I have fought my way back to safety now. I didn't mourn about her the past months. I don't want to write about these painful meaningless relationships anymore

Tuesday 11 August 2015

Had a great day, things are improving, I am now writing a bit. I was translating a couple of poems Maita Shava and Ndinorangarira from the English versions of these for a call I want to send them to

*

I wrote Maita Shava for Munashe a few months ago and she performed it on the wedding of her friend, days when we were close

*

Translating English to Shona is different from translating Shona into English. I have translated a number of Shona poems into English, it's more difficult because Shona language is different from English. There is a lot of sounds and music you have to take into consideration, plus Nyaudzosingwi, which are not in English language.

*

My brother Bernard is jailed in South African jail. I was last told it was over crimes like forgery he committed using forged documents. People have been paying money to his wife for his release but nothing is happening. We don't know what to make of it.

*

We do talk about the political situation here to make it easy for us to deal with the despondent situation here. Things are getting worse and worse, the government has no clue whatsoever on how to deal with the situation. Today in the *Zimbabwean Newspaper* online there is speculation there is a move to push 2018 elections to 2021 by the ZANUPF government, maybe to buy time to sort the economic crisis before another election they are afraid they might lose

*

We can't just brush aside and say, No, it won't happen. But with ZANUPF anything is possible. Or it's just a game, political game to disguise or unfocus the parties and electorate on the looming 2018 election

*

By the way things are going ZANUPF won't have anything to sell to the electorate by the time we get to 2018

Thursday 13 August 2015

I am on ground zero

*

I feel broken heartedness, like concrete blocks broken, wire, slush, metals, planks, shit, I feel an accumulation of piled up shit of the earthquakes, or bomb blast.

*

I feel stunted in my creativity today. I am trying to work on some stories for the next collection but feel stunted

*

It's becoming more and more warm though, maybe my body is trying to adapt to the beauty of the sun, its corrosive power.

*

I am listening to James Blunt, such sadness and pain

Monday 7 September 2015

I am beginning to realize how difficult it is to keep a diary cycle when you have so much on your platter going on. I am not finding the time or when I have the time I will be too bored to write even though there is so much in me that wants to be written. I don't have the words

*

My days are flying. I am happy, I think I am finally cured of my feeling of Munashe, maybe a bit of anger still stays, not anger really, but disappointment with her, about what happened to us

*

I have another girls, and as I promised I won't write about her, just like I haven't written much about Munashe, about anything… is this drying up my diaries?

*

I could be going to Mozambique, beginning of next month, on the 4th for some NGO work in education in Manica province. I will be part of the team doing impact analysis research and compiling the reports

*

Our essays project with Mawere is shaping up. We have enough to go by, in terms of submissions. So we have been editing. I am doing my fair share of work, editing…even more than Mawere. That will be my 7th book

*

I am mooting another anthology for this year of poetry with an Angolan poet, Daniel Joao Da Purificacao that covers poets from all over Africa in at least 3 languages (English, French and Portuguese and many African languages) and I have a publisher for it, Langaa. This is the birth of Best New African Poets Anthology series…its my idea. Daniel will help with Portuguese speaking poets and French poets. It's another Journey….

I WILL NEVER WRITE DIARIES AGAIN!

Mmap Nonfiction and Academic books

If you have enjoyed *Gathering Evidence*, consider these other fine **Mmap Nonfiction and Academic books** from *Mwanaka Media and Publishing*:

Cultural Hybridity and Fixity by Andrew Nyongesa
Tintinnabulation of Literary Theory by Andrew Nyongesa
South Africa and United Nations Peacekeeping Offensive Operations by Antonio Garcia
A Case of Love and Hate by Chenjerai Mhondera
A Cat and Mouse Affair by Bruno Shora
The Scholarship Girl by Abigail George
The Gods Sleep Through It All by Wonder Guchu
PHENOMENOLOGY OF DECOLONIZING THE UNIVERSITY: Essays in the Contemporary Thoughts of Afrikology by Zvikomborero Kapuya
Africanization and Americanization Anthology Volume 1, Searching for Interracial, Interstitial, Intersectional and Interstates Meeting Spaces, Africa Vs North America by Tendai R Mwanaka
Africa, UK and Ireland: Writing Politics and Knowledge Production Vol 1 by Tendai R Mwanaka
Writing Language, Culture and Development, Africa Vs Asia Vol 1 by Tendai R Mwanaka, Wanjohi wa Makokha and Upal Deb
Zimbolicious: An Anthology of Zimbabwean Literature and Arts, Vol 3 by Tendai Mwanaka
Drawing Without Licence by Tendai R Mwanaka
Writing Grandmothers/ Escribiendo sobre nuestras raíces: Africa Vs Latin America Vol 2 by Tendai R Mwanaka and Felix Rodriguez

Nationalism: (Mis)Understanding Donald Trump's Capitalism, Racism, Global Politics, International Trade and Media Wars, Africa Vs North America Vol 2 by Tendai R Mwanaka
It Is Not About Me: Diaries 2010-2011 by Tendai Rinos Mwanaka
Chitungwiza Mushamukuru: An Anthology from Zimbabwe's Biggest Ghetto Town by Tendai Rinos Mwanaka
The Day and the Dweller: A Study of the Emerald Tablets by Jonathan Thompson
Zimbolicious Anthology Vol 4: An Anthology of Zimbabwean Literature and Arts by Tendai Rinos Mwanaka and Jabulani Mzinyathi
Parks and Recreation by Abigail George
FAMILY LAW AND POLITICS WITH BIOLOGY AND ROYALTY IN AFRICA AND NORTH AMERICA by Peter Ateh-Afec Fossungo
Writing Robotics, Africa Vs Asia, Vol 2 by Tendai Rinos Mwanaka
Zimbolicious Anthology Vol 5: An Anthology of Zimbabwean Literature and Arts by Tendai R. Mwanaka
Love Notes: Everything is Love, An Anthology of Indigenous Languages of Africa and East Europe by Tendai R Mwanaka
Zimbolicious Anthology Vol 6: An Anthology of Zimbabwean Literature and Arts by Tendai R. Mwanaka and Chenjerai Mhondera
BATTLING LANGUAGE RIGHTS GOVERNANCE IN AFRICA: SWISSELGIANISM, UBACKISM, AND THE AMBAZONIA-CAMEROUN WAR by Peter Ateh-Afec Fossungo
Otherness and Pathology: The Fragmented Self and Madness in Contemporary African Fiction by Andrew Nyongesa
Zimbabwe: The Urgency of Now by Tendai Rinos Mwanaka

Zimbabwe: The Blame Game, Recollected essays and Non-fictions by Tendai Rinos Mwanaka

The Trick is to Keep Breathing: Covid 19 Stories From African and North American Writers, Vol 3 by Tendai Rinos Mwanaka

Recentring Mother Earth by Andrew Nyongesa

Zimbabwe: Beyond Robert Mugabe by Tendai Rinos Mwanaka

Language, Thought, Art and Existence: New and Recollected Essays and Non Fictions by Tendai Rinos Mwanaka

Experimental Writing, Africa Vs Latin America Vol 1 by Tendai Rinos Mwanaka and Ricardo Felix Rodriguez

Fixing Earth Anthology: An anthology of Africa, UK and Ireland Writers, Vol 2 by Tendai Rinos Mwanaka

Africa Must Deal with Blats for Its True Decolonisation: Unclothed Truth about Internalised Internal Colonialism by Nkwazi N. Mhango

ROYAL BURIAL AND ENTHRONEMENT IN AMBAZONIA: INTERROGATING THE RELEVANCE OF POSTCOLONIAL EDUCATION IN AFRICA by Peter Ateh-Afec Fossungo

SCHOOL BASED HIV EDUCATION AFFECTING GIRLS IN SELECTED COUNTRIES IN SUB SAHARAN AFRICA by Ivainesu Charmaine Musa

HIV AND AIDS IN ZIMBABWE: A REVIEW ON THE RELATIONSHIP BETWEEN PERCEPTION OF MASCULINITY AMONGST UNMARRIED YOUNG MEN AND THEIR SEXUAL BEHAVIORS by Lucas Kudakwashe Muvhiringi

AFRICA'S CONTEMPORARY FOOD INSECURITY: SELF-INFLICTED WOUNDS THROUGH MODERN VENI VIDI VICI AND LAND GRABBING by Nkwazi Mhango

Ayabacholization Classroom In My Life: The Longest Shortcut To University Education by Peter Ateh-Afac Fossungu
I Can't Breathe and other Essays by Zvikomborero Kapuya

Upcoming
https://facebook.com/MwanakaMediaAndPublishing/

www.ingramcontent.com/pod-product-compliance
Lightning Source LLC
Chambersburg PA
CBHW070848160426
43192CB00012B/2359